Aspect Patterns
in Colour

Joyce Hopewell

HopeWell
Knutsford, England

First published in the U.K. in 2010 by HopeWell

HopeWell
PO Box 118, Knutsford
Cheshire WA16 8TG, U.K.

Edited by Barry Hopewell

ISBN 978-0-9558339-1-5

Dedicated to

Bruno, Louise and Michael Huber, who researched and developed the theory of aspect patterns, documented in their seminal book *Aspect Pattern Astrology*.

Ackowledgements

I would like to thank those people who have agreed to let me use their charts as examples in this book.

A Huber-Style Chart

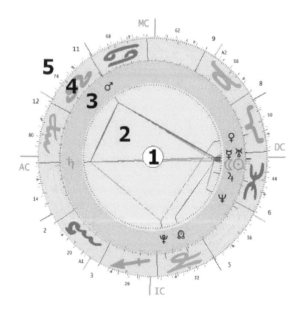

Shading to Illustrate the Five Levels

Introduction

This is a reference book about aspect patterns. It does not attempt to teach astrological psychology or explain what the birth chart is about; for this see my book *The Cosmic Egg Timer*. Also, it does not attempt to describe the theory of aspect patterns in detail; for this see Bruno & Louise Huber's book *Aspect Pattern Astrology*.

I aim to present in this book is an easy-to-use reference to the aspect patterns given by the Hubers in their book, together with an interpreted example of each individual aspect figure, using a selection of well-known people and people that I know. The interpretation is based on my own understanding and experience of many years of astrological consultancy; it should be taken in this light, and not regarded as in any sense 'the truth'.

But before you use this reference there are certain things that you need to understand, particularly if you have not previously studied astrological psychology.

The Huber-Style Chart and the Five Levels

Bruno Huber was a pioneer in the use of colour in the chart, based on his understanding of the psychology of colour. You can see an example chart opposite (above).

In astrological psychology the birth chart is interpreted in five distinct and independent levels, illustrated in the shaded chart below the example. These are the five levels:

1. The **centre circle** symbolises the inner, higher self, the central core of the person.

2. The **aspect pattern** represents inner unconscious motivation.

3. The **planets** represent our psychological drives.

4. The **signs** of the zodiac represent inherited traits and qualities.

5. The **houses** represent the environment around us, the outside world.

The basic rule is: Do not mix up the levels. Interpretive features at one level should not be mixed up with those at another level – for example, aspects are not drawn between planets and the angles (AC, DC, MC, IC) as the angles are on the level of the houses, which is separate from the level of the planets.

The Centre Circle

The circle at the centre of the chart represents our essential inner self, the unknown source of our life, identity, will and consciousness. From here, energy flows out through the aspect pattern and the planets, coloured by the signs, into the world of the houses.

The Aspect Pattern

The only aspects used in astrological psychology are those of 30 degrees, illustrated in the Ptolemaic Arrangement (below). The aspects are coloured according to their essential quality: cardinal = red, fixed = blue, mutable = green. The colour orange is used for conjunctions.

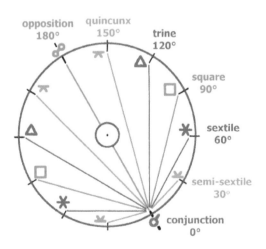

Ptolemaic Arrangement of the Aspects

Meaning of the Aspect Pattern

"This is where we look to see the unconscious driving forces of the individual. The aspects are pulsating with energy of different kinds and qualities, and the aspect structure offers valuable information about what makes us "tick", what really drives us.

The motivation shown here is largely unconscious, but we can get to know and understand it better – and we can choose to work on familiarizing ourselves with what truly makes us "tick". Anything that is unconscious, such as our inner motivation, can be brought into consciousness. We can recognise it, we can accept it and we can begin to work with it. Then we can start to transform it, change it, integrate it, and allow it to become an integrated part of our lives. Such integration and development of the 'whole' person is the aim of the approach to psychology known as psychosynthesis.

Although the motivation shown in this part of the chart might start off by being unconscious, we can thus bring it into greater awareness so that we can move forward feeling more firmly in the driving seat of our lives."

quoted from *The Cosmic Egg Timer*

Chart Image, Colour, Shaping and Direction

We can learn a lot about motivation from the perceived image, colour, shaping and direction of the aspect pattern. These are all covered in *The Cosmic Egg Timer*, so are not further explained here.

Individual Aspect Figures

Individual figures that are distinct components of the aspect pattern may consist of simply straight lines (linear – cardinal motivation), be triangular (mutable motivation) or have four or more sides (fixed motivation). This subject is introduced in *The Cosmic Egg Timer*.

Detailed rules for interpretation of individual aspect figures from first principles can be found in Bruno & Louise Huber's *Aspect Pattern Astrology* and should be understood by all serious students of this subject. It also covers important features such as the significance of incomplete aspect figures (e.g. corner gaps, missing aspects) and one-way aspects, and introduces all the aspect figures found in this book.

The Planets

Astrological psychology uses only the seven classical planets, the three outer (transpersonal) planets (including Pluto) and the Moon's North Node. In charts, the three personality or ego planets Sun (will/mind), Moon (feelings) and Saturn (body) are normally drawn in red. See table of planets and their glyphs.

Ego Planets		Tool Planets		Transpersonal Planets	
Sun	☉	Mercury	☿	Uranus	♅
Moon	☽	Venus	♀	Neptune	♆
Saturn	♄	Mars	♂	Pluto	♇
		Jupiter	♃		

ascending Moon Node ☊

The Planets and their Glyphs

Aspect Orbs

The psychological researches of the Hubers established the figures in the table below to give orbs appropriate for astrological psychology (see *Aspect Pattern Astrology*) and thus for interpretation of the aspect figures given in this book.

Planet	⬦	⌓ ✶	□	△	☌ ☍
☉ ☽	3°	5°	6°	8°	9°
☿ ♀ ♃	2°	4°	5°	6°	7°
♂ ♄	1½°	3°	4°	5°	6°
♅ ♆ ♇	1°	2°	3°	4°	5°

Aspect Orbs

The Signs of the Zodiac

The signs represent inherited traits and characteristics and influence the energy of planets contained within them. They are coloured according to their element: fire = red, earth = green, air = yellow, water = blue.

Aries	♈	♎	Libra
Taurus	♉	♏	Scorpio
Gemini	♊	♐	Sagittarius
Cancer	♋	♑	Capricorn
Leo	♌	♒	Aquarius
Virgo	♍	♓	Pisces

The Houses

The twelve houses represent our environment – the influence of family, friends, social contacts and so on. We use standard abbreviations for the angles of the chart i.e. Ascendant (AC), Descendant (DC), Imum Coeli (IC) and Medium Coeli (MC). The two hemispheres and four quadrants bounded by them have specific psychological meanings.

Bruno Huber found the **Koch House System** to be the most appropriate and reliable house system for use in astrological psychology. The meaning of the aspect patterns given in this book are not necessarily valid under any other house system.

In the interpretations in this book you may find reference to some special positions in the houses – at the house **cusp** energies are directed outwards, at the **Balance Point** inner energies and outer demands tend to be balanced, and at the **Low Point** energies are turned inward. The areas between these points are **cardinal**, **fixed** and **mutable zones**, with corresponding qualities. The latter is also known as the **stress zone** just before the next house **cusp**, where there is psychological anticipation of the next house leading to potential stress.

There is also reference to **Age Progression**, where the person's **Age Point** passes through one house in turn every six years.

All these features are introduced in *The Cosmic Egg Timer*. It is important to be aware that all these house-related features are only of significance if the birth time is accurate.

Beyond the Natal Chart

You will also find occasional reference to other features of astrological psychology that are not contained in the natal chart, in particular the House Chart and the Moon Node Chart, plus the significance of Age Progression in the latter. These are introduced in my book *The Living Birth Chart*.

Layout of this Book

The Aspect Figures

The remainder of this book is devoted to the individual aspect figures. It comprises two-page spreads, one for each figure:

> The left-hand page contains the aspect figure with a brief description.

> The right-hand page contains an example chart containing the figure within the overall aspect pattern, plus a brief and selective interpretive narrative related to the figure.

Indexes

Alphabetical and pictorial indexes to aspect figures are on pages 89-91.

Resources

Pages 93-95 list resources and book references that are available to assist your further study of aspect patterns and astrological psychology.

The Aspect Figures

To assist in use as a reference, the aspect figures are presented in colour-coded chapters as follows:

Note that all of the aspect figures given in *Aspect Pattern Astrology* appear, with the following exceptions:

The Diamond figure, which it is not likely to occur in practice.

The Buffer, Runner and Butterfly, which are incomplete versions of the Shield, Telescope and Trawler respectively.

Achievement Triangle

Efficiency Triangle

Performance Triangle

T-Square

An Achievement Triangle is a mutable, adaptable figure, but its key function is achievement through purposeful work. It has the capacity to work tirelessly because the aspects are red, and it can adapt to changing situations, moving with the flow of events yet remaining charged with cardinal "doing" energy. The opposition acts as a store for this energy, holding it in readiness, like a well-charged battery. Energy can be discharged and released along the two squares, but the planet at the apex of this figure is key, indicating where the achievement is directed, and what planetary principle is involved. This is the outlet where the energy, work, efficiency and achievement is expressed.

Queen Elizabeth the Second
21.4.1926, 02:40, London, UK

Could there be a more appropriate apex planet than Saturn for a ruling monarch? Not only is Saturn at the apex of this aspect pattern, but it also reigns at the top of the chart, strongly placed in a cuspal position right on the MC. Now in her eighties, and sovereign for over fifty five years, there has been speculation on the Queen's possible retirement. But it seems unlikely that she will stand aside for son and heir Charles. Her strong sense of duty and dedication to her role is well documented, and that firmly placed Saturn bears this out and reflects her position as head of the family firm.

The other planets involved in the Achievement Triangle hold and store the working energy and drive of this figure; Mars/Jupiter suggests an abundance of energy and Neptune indicates the possibility of this being directed towards ideal, all-inclusive goals. These planets are stressed before the 2nd and 8th house cusps so there will be an urgency and on-going drive to utilise her energy to secure and stabilise (she wants the monarchy to continue) as well as to reach out to other areas and societies (her unwavering support of the Commonwealth is well-known). Saturn's placement as the outlet planet in this figure is most significant, providing the structure, discipline and adherence to rules and traditions that she was brought up with, and ensuring that in her lifetime these do not disappear.

Achievement Square

Efficiency Square

Performance Square

Grand Cross

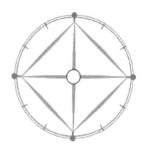

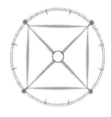

The Achievement Square is a large quadrangular figure with a fixed motivation. Being all-red it has a cardinal mode of action and embodies active energy which is used to produce and ensure stability and security. It is often found in the charts of workaholics, or in people who need to work hard in order to maintain or justify their existence. They may identify themselves solely through their capacity to work, so much so that it is difficult for them to switch off and rest. Rather than stop, people with this figure will switch the focus of their output from one of the corner apex planets to another, thus ensuring a rest for the remaining three.

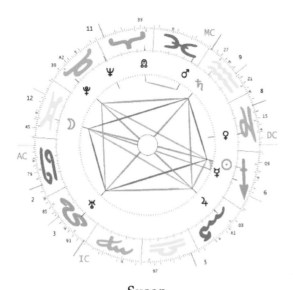

Susan
12.12.1875, 16:40, Enfield, UK

The Achievement Square dominates Susan's chart. Two pinning planets are shared with a Righteousness Rectangle; the overall impression is of the taut energy of the red oppositions inside these interconnected fixed figures – suggesting a life of work and energy expended in pursuit of security. Susan brought up six children in the early 20th century in comparative poverty. At age 20, with the birth of her first child, her Age Point was quincunx pinning Saturn. The Achievement Square is pinned by two personal and two transpersonal planets – energy will have been focussed more on Saturn and Jupiter, and less on Uranus and Pluto, as survival was paramount.

All four pinning planets are on Low Points, graphically describing her attitude of 'just getting on with it' when life was tough. Work, labour and toil were simply what life was about. In spite of this, Susan's Sagittarian Sun/Mercury shone through, and 5th house Jupiter on one corner of the square was an outlet for positive, expansive energy. There was a sense of fun, humour and optimism in the way she related to others, and she was something of an actress, singer and dancer, performing informally. Outside the square unaspected Venus and Neptune are both in earth signs, indicating the practical creative crafts she was good at. Susan was widowed suddenly and unexpectedly when her Age Point was conjunct Saturn opposite Uranus, and died as her Age Point approached conjunction with Uranus.

Talent Triangle, Large

Grand Trine

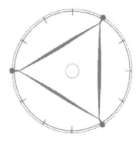

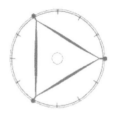

The Large Talent Triangle is an all-blue figure with a mutable motivation, making it fluid and adaptable. However, much of this flexibility may be lost or simply not tapped into, because of the lack of red aspects and the fixed nature of the blue aspects. The inherent talent in this figure may be related to the element of the signs the pinning planets are placed in. The talent concerned is already developed and in place. As the person does not need to work at it, the downside is that they may not bother to use this talent or it may simply be lost for lack of expression.

Marlon Brando, Actor

3.4.1924, 23:00, Omaha, NE, USA

Marlon Brando's Large Talent Triangle is pinned by planets in fire signs, suggesting energetic input from Jupiter and Neptune along with ego planets Sun/Moon, representing his mental and emotional sense of self. Brando was considered to be the master of method acting, a technique by which the actor draws on their own emotions, memories and life experiences when in character. His acting career began on stage but he was best known in films, often cast in powerful roles, as in *On the Waterfront* and *The Godfather*. The all-blue Large Talent Triangle needs red aspects to kick it into action; the Sun/Moon conjunction receives this via red squares to cardinal Mars and Pluto.

Jupiter on the 1st house Low Point suggests the potential for drawing on the large store of inner experiences and memories required by method acting. Neptune, at the triangle's apex, is symbolic of Brando's talent being expressed in film; it also suggests an ability to get beneath the skin of the characters played and merge with them. Neptune is also at the apex of a Projection Figure, seeking to project its energies and qualities on to the screen created by the sextile spanning the 3rd house. Brando was parodied in his early career because of his mumbling diction, perhaps related to Mercury's position near a Low Point. However, his status as movie icon and master of method acting sit most convincingly with the combination of pinning planets which give expression to the inherent ability in his Large Talent Triangle.

Talent Triangle, Small

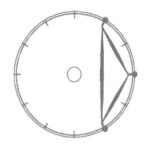

This all-blue triangular figure has a mutable motivation, making it fluid and adaptable, but within certain bounds as blue aspects have a fixed quality. No red aspects are involved, so to activate and develop the inherent talent in this pattern some connection with a red aspect is desirable for progress to be made. People with this aspect figure may choose not to stretch themselves out and explore their latent capabilities as the trine tends to be a lazy aspect. But the sextiles encourage growth, meeting at the apex planet which indicates the outlet point for the talent. For those who are willing to explore expression of their potential talents – indicated by the pinning planets – the rewards can be impressive.

Helen Mirren, Actor

26.7.1945, 02:00 , London, UK

Helen Mirren's Talent Triangle (Sun, Mars, Neptune) spans the lower hemisphere. Notably, Sun is at the apex, the outlet point, and Mars sits close to a Balance Point. Neptune on the 5th house cusp is well-placed to absorb and express all nuances in the area of relationships – an invaluable tool for an actor. As this aspect figure indicates a still-developing talent, something one has to work on, polish and perfect throughout life, it surely relates to her acting skills.

The triangle's focus in the collective area of the chart suggests a resonance and connection with the issues of everyday life. The Sun is strongly placed in the 3rd house of communication, conjunct Pluto. Over a stage and film career spanning more than 45 years, Pluto's influence can be seen; her roles have often been powerful and gritty, and she is able to bring intensity, sexuality and sensuality to the characters she plays. Growth of the talent comes from the sextiles and their pinning planets Mars and Neptune. Mars suggests the work of perfecting the craft of acting, the red aspect to Mercury giving this blue figure the energy it needs to be productive. Neptune offers absorption of impressions and feelings – vital food for an actor. Sun, at the apex, encompasses not only the direction and expression of the talent, but also her own sense of self, mind-set, creativity and determination to succeed and achieve recognition. Not for nothing is her Moon on the MC and she a star in her own right.

Ambivalence Triangle

Single Ambivalence Figure

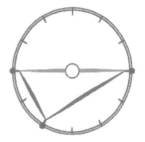

The Ambivalence Triangle, being triangular, has mutable motivation. It can be flexible, adapting to change as needed. Composed of only red/blue aspects, it operates in an either/or manner. The red aspect is concerned with work whilst the blue aspects provide opportunities to relax. The planet at the point where the blue aspects meet can be the escape point as the person will use and express the qualities of this planet when they switch off from work, relax and do something they enjoy. The ambivalence in this figure comes from its work/rest cycle of behaviour; when in work mode the person will want to be relaxing, and vice versa.

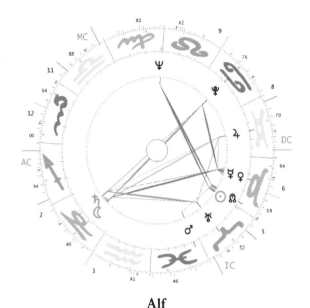

Alf

19.04.1930, 23:20, Croft near Wainfleet, UK

Alf's Ambivalence Triangle has the red opposition across the 2/8 axis, concerned with possessions. In the fixed 2nd house, the Saturn/ Moon conjunction in Capricorn suggests a formidable ability to hold on to all that is held dear and is essential for survival. Their opposition to Pluto in the 8th hints at constant hard work and perhaps meeting the demands of society as a balance is sought between personal and shared possessions. At the escape point on the "You" side, Mercury/Venus offer pleasant diversion from the realities of work. This tight conjunction signifies communication, mental stimulation, companionship, friends, appreciation of beauty and good taste – a complete contrast to the demands of the 2/8 axis.

Alf grew up in the 1930s, the only child of a widow managing on a small pension. Some help was given, e.g. food, by members of the village community, but his childhood was dominated by make-do-and-mend, recycling anything that could aid survival. Saturn/Moon symbolises the symbiotic mother/child relationship, Pluto the drive to transform in order to survive. Escape and relief came via Mercury/ Venus; the village Christmas party, the annual Sunday School outing to the seaside. Alf's adult working life as teacher and lecturer included worldwide contacts and friendships, with appreciation of modest luxuries he knew little of as a child. Now retired, he is more often found enjoying and expressing the escape planets in this figure.

Cradle

The Cradle is a blue/red quadrangular figure. Motivated towards stability and security, it is a very stable structure. Like a baby's cradle, it provides a safe refuge where the individual can snuggle down in the safety and comfort of the blue aspects. The red opposition acts as a protective barrier, behind which the person can hide. With two Small Talent Triangles as component parts of this figure, the talent is there to be tapped into and developed. The person, however, has to overcome their fear of falling out of the Cradle into the opposite empty area of the chart. Their task is to leave the security of the Cradle, go into the empty space and creatively express their inherent talent.

Jimi Hendrix, Musician, Singer, Songwriter

27.11.1942, 10:15, Seattle, WA, USA

Jimi Hendrix's chart is dominated by a Cradle in the upper hemisphere. Apart from one green aspect, the red/blue chart suggests an all or nothing approach to life. Hendrix is considered to be amongst the greatest electric guitarists in the history of rock music. He was influential in the 1960s across a range of styles. His Cradle is pinned by ego planets Sun and Moon, both conjunct tool planets, plus Uranus and Neptune. At the blue-only corners, Moon/Jupiter and Neptune have the capacity to be receptive as well as focussed on enjoyment; Hendrix's well-documented use of drugs and alcohol is one manifestation. His talent and creativity came out in many ways.

With innovative input from Uranus he created something unique – the flair shown in flamboyant clothes, song lyrics and a distinctive musical style. Using his creativity he was able to move away from the safety of the Cradle and make contact, through music, with the empty collective area of the chart. He was successful and iconic. It could be argued that the need to escape the realities of life outside the Cradle, and retreat to the safety of the blue behind the red opposition, was expressed in his drug and alcohol use. With such an emphasised upper hemisphere it is never easy to stay grounded; the Hubers describe a Cradle here as being like a parachute, ungrounded and rootless. One of Hendrix's compositions, *Valleys of Neptune*, reflects this with Neptune as his highest planet.

Kite

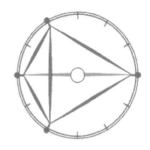

The Kite is a quadrilateral, motivated towards security. With only red and blue aspects, it may operate in an on/off manner, seeking to intersperse periods of rest in the blue aspects with a somewhat tense approach to the work that needs to be completed in the red opposition. This figure contains large quantities of talent (its component parts include two Talent Triangles) but the individual may prefer not to tap into this and produce something until they absolutely have to. The Kite is found in the charts of artists and creative people, who often go right to the wire when producing to a deadline. They may find it easier to stay in the blue part of this figure until close to the deadline, when the red finally kicks in.

Elton John, Musician and Singer

29.03.1947, 16:00, Pinner, UK

The Hubers say in *Aspect Pattern Astrology* that people with a Kite have a certain charisma, and may also be hedonistic. Elton John's chart is dominated by a vertical Kite. Since the early 1970s when his recording career took off, he has always been flamboyant, with a distinctly Jupiterian style to his dress and performances. Jupiter plays a key role at the Kite's tail; in the 4th house and close to the IC it roots him in the collective, speaking of his popularity over several decades. Jupiter is in opposition to the North Node in the 10th house, at the aspiration point of the figure – which the individual can develop and grow towards as the inherent talent in the small triangle is developed. A 10th house Node suggests the task is to overcome his fears of standing alone as an individual. The overall fixed structure of John's chart, indicating a need for security, might easily have pulled him back to the comparative safety of the South Node conjunct Jupiter.

Jupiter at the tail could represent a psychological drive holding back growth; the lavish costumes, excessive amounts of money reputedly spent on flowers and ownership of a football club could all be expressions of this. However, Sun and Saturn are strongly placed by house at the Kite's arms, contributing sound sense and structure. They bring balance and moderation to Jupiter's possible excesses, promoting long term development of the aspiration point, and allowing this Kite to fly successfully.

Righteousness Rectangle

Mystic Rectangle

The Righteousness Rectangle is a red/blue figure with a fixed motivation. Enclosed entirely by the blue aspects visible to the environment, the impression given is of calm, serenity and harmony. In contrast, the tension created by the red oppositions is concealed within this contained space; if it were possible to step inside it would feel like being caught in the crossfire between two opposing factions. Some people with this figure deny that there are such things as problems because they do not want to look inside and resolve their own. Others, however, are willing to do this and work, with awareness, on overcoming them.

Jean Paul Sartre, Philosopher and Author

21.06.1905, 19:35, Paris, France

Jean-Paul Sartre's red and blue chart is dominated by a Righteousness Rectangle spanning axes 2/8 and 3/9. Sun/Mercury opposite Uranus and Saturn opposite the Moon's Node form the internal red crossfire. The intercepted Moon's Node points to an area of life worth exploring, an important step on the path of self-awareness; it is significantly in the 9th house for this leading existential philosopher. Saturn in the 3rd house, in opposition to the Node, provides the practical means for grounding and expressing his work in concrete form: his writing. He was also a novelist, playwright, screenwriter, biographer and literary critic, who refused the Nobel Prize for Literature in 1964.

Sartre the writer can be seen in his Sun/Mercury conjunction in Gemini. The added weight of Neptune and Pluto flanking this conjunction give his thought, writing and subject matter depth and intensity. Uranus in the 1st house opposite brings not only flashes of insight and leaps of intellect, but describes his unconventional attitudes, lifelong Marxism and ongoing challenge of bourgeois values. If the highest level for the Righteousness Rectangle is to transcend the inner conflict of the oppositions, and live at ease with both the red and blue of this pattern, then Sartre lived much of his life in this way. He said, "I would like people to remember the milieu or historical situation in which I lived... how I lived it, in terms of all the aspirations which I tried to gather up within myself."

Irritation Triangle

Irritation Triangles have a mutable motivation and are composed of red and green aspects, making them touchy, tetchy, sensitive figures with a surfeit of nervous energy. They are seen in the charts of people who are flexible, hard working, and sensitively aware. These people can often take on more than their fair share of work, but sometimes they take on too much, reach breaking point and explode. Those around them take cover until the storm passes, and then things calm down quickly as the person returns to what they were doing, feeling a whole lot better having worked both angst and irritation out of their system with the outburst, and cleared the air.

Clint Eastwood, Actor

31.05.1930, 17:35, San Francisco, CA, USA

Clint Eastwood's chart lacks blue aspects to help offset the sensitivity of the high red/green ratio. He has starred in and directed films for many years, seemingly tirelessly, which is not difficult to understand considering this colour balance. Taken together, the emphasised red/green colour balance and the red/green Irritation Triangle with its opposition on the 2/8 Possessions Axis start to offer a theme throwing some light on his motivation. Also notable is the large Learning Triangle attached to this figure; the two figures could work in a complementary way. Uranus in the Learning Triangle suggests a creative or innovative approach, borne out in two of his best rated films, *Million Dollar Baby* and *Gran Torino*, as well as in the surreal *High Plains Drifter*.

In 1971 Eastwood's Age Point was conjunct Sun, picking up the Irritation Triangle as he made his debut as a director as well as starring in the film *Play Misty for Me*. The same year, he starred in the first *Dirty Harry* film, a character which became his signature role. His achievements in the film world are impressive. Saturn, a pinning planet of the Irritation Triangle, is out on a limb, on its own in the 2nd house. In its ruling sign Capricorn, Saturn will be at home with grounding and making things manifest as well as having an eye on stability and security within the fixed, quadrangular structure it is a part of. With only red and green aspects, it too will be active, sensitive, aware, and practical.

Irritation Rectangle

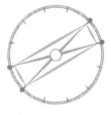

The Irritation Rectangle is a red/green quadrangular figure with a fixed motivation. Externally all that can be seen are green aspects, giving the impression that the person can be adaptable and flexible, but also bound up in thought and the pursuit of ideas. Inside, the oppositions tell a different story. There is a lot of internal strife and conflict which the person seeks to mask with the sensitive green outer aspects. The Hubers say in *Aspect Pattern Astrology* that "the person learns early on to defend himself against attack, which makes real contact with him difficult." They conclude, "The Irritation Rectangle requires that inner tension be used as the impetus for personal development."

Louise

15.12.1975, 19:15, Orpington, UK

Louise's Irritation Rectangle is separate from the other aspects in her chart. It spans the 4/10 Individuality and 5/11 Relationship axes, indicating sensitivity, awareness and information seeking in these areas of life. The presence of Sun and Moon in this figure suggests its significance; overcoming issues about her sense of self and asserting herself in relationships may be central to her development. She will use the outer green aspects in the rectangle to pick up information, body language, verbal and visual clues from the environment. But rather than bending to demands and pressures, she will tend to remain steady and keep them under control (this is a fixed figure).

Internally things may be different. The conflict of the oppositions could be felt but not expressed. Sun and Mars, in opposition on the Relationship Axis, are on Balance Points, so can work effectively in the world, but she may rein in her assertiveness, particularly in relationships. Moon in 10th is highly placed but intercepted, so relies on planets aspected for pathways into the world. This could mean that her emotional responses are dampened, misunderstood or not heard. Louise may not always be acknowledged as an individual in her own right, which could be frustrating. Moon's Node in 4th, once consciously activated, can help point the way forward, with Louise's need for stability met by nurturing a safe base and creating a sense of belonging and security.

Information Triangle

Eye

Ear

This small triangular pattern both looks and acts like a tiny radar dish. It is highly sensitive to picking up and storing all manner of information from the surrounding environment. It gathers this in effortlessly, storing it away for future use. The Information Triangle has a mutable motivation and no red aspects, but it works well on its own. The green semi-sextiles continuously absorb information, facts, clues, hints, words and visual impressions from the surroundings. These are stored in the blue sextile aspect, ready to be accessed when the need arises. The area of the chart that this figure spans will be the one from which the information is gathered.

Anne Frank, Diarist

12.06.1929, 07:30, Frankfurt am Main, Germany

As a teenager, Anne Frank and her family went into hiding in Amsterdam to avoid the persecution of Jews under the Nazi occupation. The family lived in hidden rooms at the rear of her father's office building for two years. Anne called these rooms 'The Secret Annexe', shown graphically in the Information Triangle spanning the 12th house with Pluto, keeper of secrets, at its apex. The Frank family were joined by several others in this hiding place, and Anne began writing her now famous diary. Using the Information Triangle to draw on observations of her fellow inmates, she wrote about her relationships with the members of her family and their personalities. She described the other people sharing this secret space, noting many small details about them and painting vivid word pictures of the facilities they shared.

Anne wanted to become a journalist, symbolised by Gemini Sun conjunct Mercury. Cardinal Sun, Mars and Pluto give her Information Triangle active energy and drive. Pluto in 12th speaks of secrets observed and of a sequestered life. The attached Small Learning Triangle suggests that Anne used the information gathered in a focused way. She wrote, "if I don't have the talent to write books or newspaper articles, I can always write for myself, but will I ever be able to write something great, will I ever become a journalist or a writer?" Anne's legacy to humanity is her diary. Her words and observations live on, reaching way beyond her early, untimely death.

Projection Triangle

Finger of God/Fate

Yod

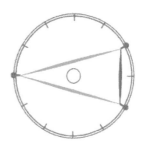

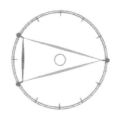

The aspect colours and motivation of this triangular, mutable figure are blue and green. No cardinal red aspects are involved. The blue sextile provides substance; the green quincunxes bring searching and questing qualities, the ability to seek for answers and aim long-term for goals, underpinned with considerable awareness and sensitivity. This figure is known as the Projection Triangle, not because of an association with the psychological term "projection", but because the whole figure works like a slide- or film-projector. The planet at the apex is the projection source, which transmits its qualities down the sensitive green quincunxes to the blue sextile which forms the screen. The screen receives and makes the imagined images visible, but always according to the planets which pin each end.

Meryl Streep, Actor

22.06.1949, 08:05, Summit, NJ, USA

The Projection Triangle, the only complete aspect figure in Meryl Streep's chart, dominates the horizontal axis where encounters take place. At the apex, Jupiter is the projection source, transmitting its qualities down the quincunxes to the blue sextile screen. The screen makes the imagined images visible, according to the planets at its ends – Saturn and the tight Sun/Uranus conjunction. Positioned as it is with the direction moving from Jupiter near the DC to Sun/Uranus and Saturn on the AC side of the chart, this figure could lead to giving too much importance to the opinions of others.

It could easily be argued that this figure, with its connotations of screen and projector, would make life a cinch for a film actor, but it is not as simple as that. In charts with this figure what has to be considered is whether projections are made consciously or unconsciously. In view of Streep's maturity, breadth of experience and success as an actor, it is most likely that she is using this figure consciously, as doing so would be of enormous value to her in the acting roles she undertakes. With a track record of countless awards for her performances, including Oscars, the influence of meticulous Saturn, concerned as ever with form and here pinning the screen of the Projection Triangle, is almost certainly at work.

Search Triangle

Search figures are triangular, and thus have a mutable motivation, behaving fluidly rather than rigidly. Composed solely of green and blue aspects, they are bound up with thought, ideas and an ongoing search which has an "if only I can find the answer to such and such, I will be happy and satisfied" quality. The search is the spur and the drive. The Hubers say in *Aspect Pattern Astrology* that people with this figure "are suited to working on long-term projects and can wait patiently until success comes of its own accord. They work continuously with the same dedication as at the start and know that everything takes time." Experience suggests that the planet at the blue/green corner of this figure is the one which offers possible outlets and expression for the searching involved.

Charles Darwin, Naturalist

12.02.1809, 03:00 (time unreliable), Shrewsbury, UK

The quote opposite aptly describes Darwin's scientific study of evolution. His chart contains two Search Triangles, crossing over each other like crossed green/blue daggers. One figure is pinned by Saturn/Neptune, Uranus/Node and Venus; the other, which is part of the larger quadrangular Surfer figure, is pinned by Sun, Jupiter and Mars. Both figures have adjacent red aspects which offer cardinal energy to help activate what has been absorbed and learned during the search.

There is a scientific flavour to both figures, with Darwin's Aquarian Sun in one and both Saturn and Uranus in the other. The planets at the blue/green outlet corners are his Aquarian Sun and the Saturn/Neptune conjunction. Uranus is also involved, representing creative and scientific thought. Uranus is the researcher who breaks boundaries and seeks new horizons; Saturn the methodical scientist who grounds and forms the theories. An Aquarian Sun is unlikely to want to be pinned down, and if the Sun is working at a conscious level within the individual there will be a strong urge to explore ideas in a creative way. The presence of Jupiter in one of the Search Figures, and Darwin's lengthy voyage of exploration on board HMS Beagle, reflects his drive to study, search and eventually form and propagate his theory of evolution.

Decorative Figure

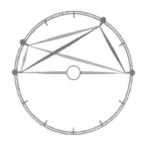

The Decorative Figure, quadrangular and containing all three aspect colours, is alert and awake, able to decode information and present it in clear, plain language. This figure seeks perfection. Described by the Hubers in *Aspect Pattern Astrology* as able to "convert tension into harmony, unite the ugly and the beautiful and break hard truths gently", people with this figure have a unique receptivity to moods, attitudes and atmospheres, and doggedly seek solutions to problems. The wedge-like shape of the Decorative Figure means that it can act as a battering ram; the Hubers say that those with this figure are "tough, and give intensely".

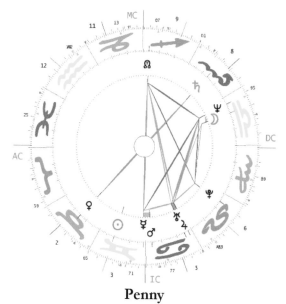

Penny

01.06.1955, 02:30, Knowle, UK

Penny describes her experience of this figure in graphic terms, agreeing that she has great tenacity. She can be very determined and will not give up until she finds a solution to a problem. She likes to put things right. When what begins as a random set of circumstances takes shape and falls into place, then the perfection desired by the Decorative Figure is reached; she is satisfied and can move on. Penny relates the semi-sextile between Mercury/Mars and Jupiter/Uranus, in the collective area of the chart, to her work in the fields of technology and communications. The information pulsing between the two intelligence planets is given additional energy and creative drive by Mars and Uranus.

Moon/Neptune in Libra are tools used to seek the harmony this figure aspires to. Penny has an idealised view of life where everyone works for the good of all. She uses these planets to sense clues from others, such as body language and listening for what is not said. The Moon's Node in this figure at the top of the chart on the MC presents a challenge. She is aware of the comfort of Mercury/South Node in opposition, and strives to balance her own need to develop, which will take her away from this area towards her own individuality. Penny says, "Given that the Decorative Figure can be a bit of a bulldozer I will no doubt continue to move unstoppably on until I get the solution I am looking for. And hopefully I'll pass it on to others in the process, as this figure is geared to do."

Learning Triangle, Dominant

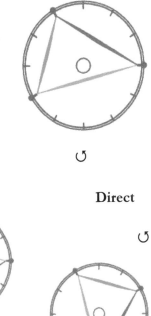

↺

Direct

↺

Retrograde ↻

↻

The Dominant Learning Triangle covers a large area of the chart enclosing the central core. With mutable motivation, its drive is for growth and movement. The person with this figure in their chart is a lifelong learner. With all three aspect colours present, each learning journey around the triangle presents new opportunities for deepening understanding and acquiring new perspectives and abilities, depending on the pinning planets. As with all Learning Triangles, the activity and the learning process begins with the dynamic red square, provoked by tension with the planet at the red/blue corner, and progresses via the green quincunx to the blue trine. If this process runs anticlockwise (direct), the learning process is much faster than if it runs clockwise (retrograde); in the latter case lessons may have to be learned again and again.

Bill Gates, Entrepreneur

28.10.1955, 22:00, Seattle, WA, USA

In Bill Gates' chart the learning process begins with Uranus in the cardinal zone of the 1st house. Uranus here could be a source of inspiration, ideas and leaps of insight; it is also associated with innovative technology. An original idea coming from Uranus demands action, so the red "doing" square between Uranus and Sun is activated, and his mind, will and ability to make decisions are brought into play. Being a Scorpio Sun, these qualities are not shallow or superficial and there may be shrewd strategy involved. Action has been initiated, but then searching, questing, mutable qualities become involved as the learning process travels along the green quincunx to the Moon to test out the feel of the whole thing.

Moon in Aries is the tension ruler of the chart, high in the 10th house near the MC. Here, for the individual, recognition of achievements is important. The journey along the final side of this figure is via the Moon-Uranus trine. The trine denotes a sense of achievement and the coming to fruition of the original idea, but there is a possible hesitancy and doubt here shown by the one-way (dotted) nature of this aspect. The learning process may end with another question mark, starting the whole process off again, maybe in a completely different way. The direction of this process is anticlockwise ('direct'), reflecting the evident ability of Gates to learn quickly.

Learning Triangles –
Large, Medium, Small

Small

Large

Medium

Small

The smaller Learning Triangles work in a similar way to the Dominant Learning Triangle, but are found around the periphery of the chart and do not enclose the central core. They are concerned with learning specific skills and the area of the chart that they span will be where this learning will take place, and be applied. Composed of all three aspect colours, the longest aspect shows which part of the learning process is most important. Red longest indicates the activity of learning; green longest shows learning takes place for the sheer joy of learning, and with blue longest, the completion of the learning task will give the greatest satisfaction. As for Dominant Triangles, the direction may be direct or retrograde, with the corresponding meaning.

Aung San Suu Kyi, Politician

19.06.1945, 12:00 (time not available), Rangoon, Burma

Aung San Suu Kyi has a Large and a Small Learning Triangle. The mutable motivation of triangles enables the person to adapt to changing circumstances. Dr. Suu Kyi, president-elect of Burma and leader of the Burmese Democracy Movement, has been kept under house arrest for almost two decades by the military government. Both triangles share the Venus/Mars conjunction in Taurus, suggesting a powerful and tenacious ability to assert herself in a non-aggressive manner. She is a Buddhist, strongly influenced by Gandhi's philosophy of non-violence. She was awarded the Nobel Peace Prize in 1991.

The Small Learning Triangle has the red square as its longest aspect, so the work involved in the learning task will be of most significance. With this retrograde triangle, associated lessons may be challenging; for instance harnessing the energy of Mars and Pluto and discovering how to ground and express these successfully through Saturn. The direct Large Learning Triangle has the green quincunx as the longest aspect, indicating the learning itself is of most importance here; Suu Kyi has studied philosophy, politics, and economics at universities in India, UK and USA, and has a natural talent for languages. She is also a powerful orator. Suu Kyi spends much of her time under house arrest reading biographies and books on philosophy and politics, perhaps focussing on the larger of the triangles.

Shield

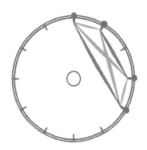

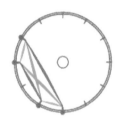

Shields are relatively rare. This quadrangular figure has all three aspect colours present and its fixed motivation is emphasised by the internal red struts which enable it to act in a defensive way to keep others at a distance. The Shield is rigid and one can imagine someone with this figure holding it up in front of themselves to repel attackers. Shields absorb incoming energy using the blue aspects, whereas the green aspects give sensitivity. Because of this they do not like people approaching them from this more vulnerable side position. The Shield can receive knocks, but beware – it can hit back strongly too.

Harriet

22.11.1954, 21:00, Birkenhead, UK

Harriet's Shield looks out to the 1st quadrant, which is concerned with survival. Pinning Pluto is stressed before the 2nd house cusp. Powerful and defensive behaviour could result if she feels her security is threatened. The green semi-sextiles, where Harriet is most likely to experience vulnerability, span the AC area and the four intercepted planets in 4th house Scorpio. There is an incomplete Achievement Triangle; the "crossed swords" effect of the Sun on one corner of the Shield not meeting up with the intercepted stellium in Scorpio to form the apex suggests inner and deeply felt frustration. This could be weighted with the negative traits of Saturn in Scorpio, the Shield then forcefully coming into action when she feels threatened.

Harriet comes from an entrepreneurial family, with siblings who have established themselves in business. A family disagreement over a business matter, involving legal action, created a schism with Harriet as the central figure. Attacked by family members, she consistently defended herself, standing behind her Shield to survive the onslaught. She became inscrutable. In *Aspect Pattern Astrology*, the Hubers say that people with the Shield keep others away "by a threatening gesture or by complaining or accusing others," which describes Harriet's approach. They add, "...this figure is much more resilient than people expect," but in Harriet's case the vulnerability is also present, with her loss of family contact.

Streamer

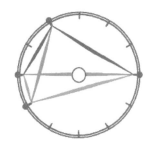

A streamer is a long, narrow flag or strip of paper which is coiled until thrown in a specific direction. The Streamer figure has its own direction, the leading planet at the corner with long aspects pointing the way. All three aspect colours are present, giving potential for growth. The Streamer can choose the direction it takes, but its goal will be to learn, communicate and acquire information. Externally, someone with a Streamer may be laid back and imaginative in the blue part of the figure and thoughtful in the green. The internal red aspects will create conflict on the opposition, with a restless urge to be active using the square.

Mike

04.01.1944, 18:00, Heswall, UK

Mike's Streamer is connected to a Bijou, giving the chart an overall blue/green emphasis, suggesting imaginative and creative potential. The only red aspects are within the Streamer. The opposition on the 5/11 Relationship Axis indicates internal tension and lessons to be learned in this area of life. The figure includes Dominant and Small Learning Triangles, so ongoing learning will be an integral part of life. Sagittarian Venus, strongly placed in 5th, leads the way, streaming towards contact with others. Mike's Moon, part of the Streamer and the chart's highest planet, is intercepted and will seek an outlet via aspected planets. With the red square to 1st house Pluto, feelings may be powerful and/or controlled.

Mike designed and built his own house, writing a published book on how to do it. His varied career includes teaching, retail, and counselling. His counselling posts have required managerial skills and he speaks of being pulled (unfurling like a streamer?) in the direction of blending caring and people-management roles in one job. Here Venus as the Streamer's leading planet, held in tension opposite Uranus/Mars in 11th, begins to make sense. The ability to relate skilfully, using Venus, is vital for successful counselling; the ability to be assertive, stand firm and be forward looking, using Uranus/Mars, is important in a managerial role. With these attributes combined, the opposition is resolved and the Streamer can fly.

43

Telescope

Microscope

Telescope

Microscope

Whether this figure is being used as a Telescope or a Microscope depends on its orientation. As a Microscope the long green quincunx is uppermost; as a Telescope, the small semi-sextile is higher. All three aspect colours are present in equal ratio, and having red/green external aspects the figure is sensitive. Being quadrangular it is security-motivated, with the inner blue aspects absorbing and processing what is learned. The green aspects act as receptive membranes, picking up information. When acting as a Telescope distant things can be observed and interconnections made. When acting as a Microscope things close to hand are seen in minute detail and the bigger picture may be lost.

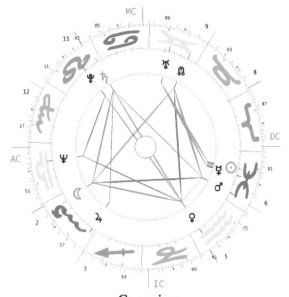

Georgina
10.03.1947, 19:10, Leeds, UK

Georgina's Microscope has its lens focussed on the 5th house, so this area of life is important to her. Friendships, contacts and relationships play a big role in her life and she is good at keeping in touch with people and extending her circle of acquaintances. Cuspal Venus and Mars strong in 6th pin the Microscope's lens, ensuring that she both receives and initiates contact. She often socialises with friends, enjoying a variety of pursuits with them. The inclusion of the Moon in her Microscope suggests that some of her emotional needs are met through such friendships.

Georgina's Microscope works in a gentle way, gathering and processing information picked up via the semi-sextile. But she can be tenacious when pursuing specific information, such as finding the best deal on a holiday or gathering facts on making optimum use of her savings; after all, Venus is opposite Saturn! In *Aspect Pattern Astrology*, the Hubers say: "Irrespective of the planets involved, this figure is characterised by a very good memory." Georgina would deny that she has a good memory, but experience suggests that she does have an ability to recall small details, long-forgotten by others. There speaks the semi-sextile working as the lens of the Microscope. The figure can be transformed to act also as a Telescope; in Georgina's chart this would involve activation of and conscious work on the 9th house North Node.

Trapeze

Large, and with a fixed motivation, the Trapeze dominates and fills most of the chart. Composed of intersecting Learning Triangles, all three aspect colours are present. This is a powerful, wide awake figure, with a huge inner capacity to think, learn and develop new ideas. The green quincunxes constantly process information and churn it around inside the large red/blue container, creating new points of view or the solution to problems. In *Aspect Pattern Astrology* the Hubers say people with a Trapeze are "…usually dominant within a group, where they serve as a role model and must accept the responsibility that goes with it."

Vladimir Putin, Politician

07.10.1952, 09:30, St Petersburg, Russia

Vladimir Putin, former President of the Russian Federation and now its Prime Minister, has a Trapeze in his chart. Its pinning planets in the 12th house stellium (Sun, Mercury, Saturn, Neptune) are shared with two other aspect figures. However, the Trapeze dominates and its internal thinking and learning processes will feed into the other figures. Strong multiple aspects from the stellium radiate out to the other pinning planets – red squares to Uranus, green quincunxes to Jupiter and blue trines to the Moon's Node. But it is the stellium that holds the eye and indicates a formidable driving force of his will (Sun), his need for firm structure (Saturn), his ability to communicate (Mercury) and his ideals (Neptune) which drive this Trapeze along. Putin has headed the direction and mindset of Russia in the 21st century. He is credited with bringing political stability and re-establishing the rule of law, yet corruption is also said to have increased.

The Hubers describe someone with a Trapeze as having "a larger-than-life personality". On the one hand, we have the outgoing Putin engaging with world leaders using Jupiter in 7th linked to Mercury, Saturn and Neptune. On the other hand there is the more inscrutable Putin with his strong-by-sign Sun dominating from the 12th, a master mind who controls and manipulates, pulling the strings like an arch puppeteer.

47

UFO

Unidentified Flying Objects are a mysterious phenomenon and there is doubt over whether they actually exist. The UFO is a quadrilateral, showing only laid back blue/green aspects externally, but internally it has strong red squares, acting as struts like crossed swords. The Hubers say in *Aspect Pattern Astrology*, "The blue-green shell behaves like a chameleon that changes colour to match the environment... deep in the heart there is a powerful store of energy, and the two intersecting blades demonstrate its invincibility." This figure can take on all comers in the belief that nobody can do it better than they can. The UFO also comprises four interlocking Learning Triangles, implying a varied capacity for learning.

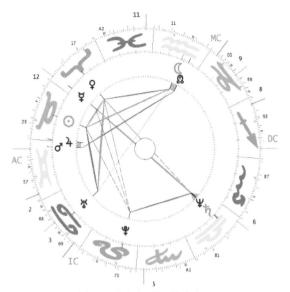

Tony Blair, Politician

06.05.1953, 06:10, Edinburgh, Scotland

Former UK Prime Minister Tony Blair's UFO spans the "I" side of his chart. The overall structure looks like a lop-sided parasol, a pram with its hood up, a helmet with visor. The impression given is of needing to protect and shield his inner sanctum and have a clear escape route away from the demands of the outside world via the 12th house Sun. All pinning planets of the UFO receive red, green and blue aspects, giving Sun, Moon, Venus and Uranus the potential to respond in an all-round way – with energy, enjoyment and sensitivity.

The Sun can make decisions, but being intercepted relies on aspected planets to be the conduit for them. Using information gathered via the semi-sextile, it can be expressed in a forthright but charming way through Venus in Aries. Uranus offers a more unpredictable route; a developed and conscious sense of self is required to handle the energy of transpersonal planets. The Moon provides the most rewarding outlet for Blair's intercepted Sun; as the highest planet it indicates the need for recognition. People with such a Moon have a sense of their own importance, expect others to look up to and admire them and are reluctant to move out of the limelight. The Hubers say that people with a UFO have a strength of will which enables them to convince others on specific issues. Blair convinced the UK parliament to go to war with Iraq, but it was later revealed that the information he based his argument on was flawed.

Animated Figure

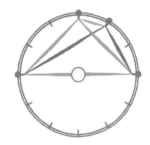

The Animated Figure is quadrangular, motivated to provide security for the individual, and has all three aspect colours present. It is composed of two Small Learning Triangles, a Single Ambivalence Figure and an Achievement Triangle. When combined together in the Animated Figure the potential exists for experiential learning and the acquisition of skills, combined with an intermittent on/off engagement with the productive work of the all-red part of the figure. The person could flip-flop between active and passive modes of action. The planet at the red apex will seek to be the outlet, but it will be sensitised by the presence of the green semi-sextile.

Henri de Toulouse-Lautrec, Artist

24.11.1864, 06:00, Albi, France

In *Aspect Pattern Astrology*, the Animated Figure is seen as reflecting "the profession of the animator. In cartoons he shows all the movement of a character... which requires imagination, patience and a lot of hard work." At age 8, as Age Point approached Venus at the red apex, Toulouse-Lautrec showed talent in drawing sketches and caricatures and, because physical disabilities prevented a more active lifestyle, immersed himself in art. He became a painter, illustrator and lithographer of the Post-Impressionist, Art Nouveau movement. His work records facets of late 19th century bohemian life in Paris.

Venus at the red apex suggest that both art and relationships were important – evident in his friendships with fellow artists (including Van Gogh) and the performers at the *Moulin Rouge* depicted candidly in his drawings, and in the bold colours in his paintings. The Animated Figure is pinned by Sun and Moon, suggesting a strong input of emotional and mental energy. Moon is opposite Neptune; although both are 'soft' planets, the flip-flop effect of 'work or play' could have contributed, particularly with Neptune involved, to his eventual descent into alcoholism. His work was often derided by other artists, and his short stature mocked, leading him to drown his sorrows in absinthe and cognac. His prolific works live on in his detailed observations of people in their working environment, animated and colourfully brought to life.

Arena

In *Aspect Pattern Astrology*, the Arena is likened to a duelling arena, where "there is the opportunity to let both parties win: one with strength and power and the other with shrewdness and knowledge." Motivated towards stability through its quadrangular shaping, the Arena is composed of several smaller aspect figures – an Achievement Triangle, a Dominant and a Medium Learning Triangle and an Irritation Triangle. A person with an Arena has two distinct sides. They can be active and energetic in the red part of the figure, imaginative and sensitive in the blue/green corner. Their task is to find the middle ground in between.

Mohandas K. Gandhi, Political and Spiritual Leader

02.10.1869, 07:11, Porbandar, India

Mohandas Gandhi was a leader in bringing independence to India. He practised non-violence in his quest for civil rights and dedicated his life to living by the principles of truth, love, simplicity and faith. The Arena has Moon and Neptune at the ends of the blue trine connecting its red and green sides. Neptune in 6th with blue/green aspects suggests the principles of faith and love in action through his selfless dedication in the service of others; Moon in 10th is the channel by which this was recognised. Jupiter/Pluto in 7th enabled him to take a stand for truth and justice, which he did throughout his life, first as a lawyer and more famously through his leadership of large-scale non-violent civil disobedience to gain human rights in South Africa and India.

The opposition on the Encounter Axis provides the greatest challenge. A balance has to be found between the personal and more indulgent manifestations of Venus/Mars in 1st and the Jupiter/Pluto principles of truth and justice in 7th. Only then can the individual stand aside from personal issues to help others in situations of conflict. The Hubers say of the Arena, "the person always puts himself in the middle between two conflicting parties... he creates suitable relationships for both opponents and helps them get over the conflict." In the campaign for Indian independence, Gandhi worked in this way, always wanting those of the Hindu and Moslem faiths to live peaceably side by side.

Double Ambivalence Figure

Ambivalence Quadrangle

The Double Ambivalence Figure covers a large area of the chart. Quadrangular with a fixed, security-seeking motivation, all three aspect colours are present, offering a balanced blend of energies. The green quincunx brings the possibility of awareness and of breaking out from what could be an endless round of work in the red area of the figure, and rest in the opposing blue. Depending on the accuracy of the angles and planetary orbs, the quincunx may not always be present. In charts where it is absent, the person may be polarised between active and passive modes. The presence of the green diagonal is beneficial and helps the individual cultivate relationships and communication.

Yitzak Rabin, Politician

01.03.1922, 12:00 (birth time unkown), Jerusalem

A Double Ambivalence Figure covers a large area in the chart of
Yitzhak Rabin, assassinated Prime Minister of Israel and holder of the
Nobel Peace Prize. Pinned by ego planets Moon and Saturn, the Mars-
Pluto quincunx links the red and blue sides of the figure. In *Aspect
Pattern Astrology* the Hubers say, "People with a Double Ambivalence
figure almost always fluctuate from one state to another." Rabin, as
Minister for Defence, took harsh measures against the first Palestinian
uprising, expressing the more formidable qualities of Pluto and Saturn
in the red area of the figure.

Later, in his second term of office as Prime Minister, Rabin played a
leading role in the signing of the Oslo Accords, creating a framework
for future cooperation between Israel and Palestine. He worked
on this with Palestinian leader Yasser Arafat and US President Bill
Clinton. Here the potential of the quincunx can be seen at work as
communication was fostered and relationships cultivated. Pluto and
Mars were able to work effectively and with awareness, bringing
together the red and blue sides of the Double Ambivalence Figure.
At the same time the higher qualities of both planets were expressed:
the leadership and courage of Mars and the transformative power of
Pluto. However, Rabin's actions split Israeli society. He was seen by
some as a hero, by others as a traitor and was assassinated in 1995.

Provocative Figure

One meaning of the word "provoke" is to irritate and annoy, yet it also means to call forth, awaken and encourage – literally to speak in favour of. The Provocative Figure can work in both ways and it will depend on the individual person how they manifest its potential. Fixed in motivation, this figure will use the red Achievement Triangle to achieve and manifest what has been stimulated by thought. Its capacity for creative ideas in the blue/green part of the figure is considerable; its nervous energy and the drive to be always "doing" is manifested in the red/green aspects. In *Aspect Pattern Astrology* the Hubers say of someone with the Provocative Figure, "…this person authorises himself and has the courage to bring things into the open that would otherwise remain hidden."

Richard Llewellyn, Astrological Counsellor

14.08.1925, 06:19, Sidcup, UK

Without the influence of Richard Llewellyn's Provocative Figure, this book may not have been written. In the early 1980s Richard, finding the more conventional approaches to astrology no longer satisfying, studied astrological psychology with Bruno & Louise Huber in Switzerland and went on to found an English-speaking school to introduce and teach the Huber Method to a worldwide audience.

Richard's Provocative Figure was instrumental in bringing forth, in the sense of provoking, the Hubers' work. Stressed Venus on the 2nd cusp is opposite strongly placed Uranus in 8th – fixed planets on the fixed 2/8 axis indicating a drive to establish foundations. Experienced at running his own businesses, Richard applied his skills to founding an astrology school, a graphic expression of Uranus in 8th. The blue/green planets Sun/Neptune in Leo fuelled creative ideas in the contemplative 12th house. His intercepted Moon, together with Venus and Uranus worked tirelessly to make his vision manifest. The Hubers say of this figure, "Pro means to be in favour of something, in this case to assert oneself in favour of a particular thing against existing resistance." Some traditional astrologers were initially resistant to a new school teaching astrological psychology, but Richard's commitment and determination to speak up for and promote this unique approach to chart interpretation means it is now an established, tried and tested method, used worldwide.

Detective

The Detective is predominantly blue/green. The single red aspect is enclosed within the figure so is not visible to the environment. It does, however, act as a driving force from within and the figure as a whole is able to absorb information from the environment (Information Triangle), to learn (Learning Triangles) and to express the talent embedded (Small Talent Triangle). The Hubers say that the Detective "can discover the smallest clue, insignificant information…" and that someone with this pattern "sticks to a trail, has a wide-awake character that nearly nothing escapes…"

Roger Federer, Tennis Player

08.08.1981, 08:40, Basel, Switzerland

The image of Roger Federer's chart suggests a hammock, swing boat, or upright pushchair with hood up. This "I" sided chart has only Neptune on the "You" side. Together with a vertical direction to the overall aspect structure, this suggests someone focussed on their own growth and self-understanding, with an urge to stand out, make a mark on the world and be recognised. The chart is blue/green with few red aspects, but this is compensated to some extent by 3 conjunctions, each with potential talent according to the planets involved. With the Detective and 4 green aspects, Federer is likely to be sensitively attuned to the surrounding environment.

Mercury conjunct Sun, both strong by sign and strongly placed on the 12th cusp, are at the apex of the Information Triangle part of the Detective. This red/green apex is the touchy part of the pattern; here one could be irritable, but Federer always appears the gentleman on and off court, often dressed stylishly in keeping with his Leo Sun. The blue Small Talent Triangle is also part of this figure. This, as well as the other components of the Detective, are what Federer seems to draw upon in competitive tennis: the ability to focus, absorb all relevant and sometimes minute details on an ongoing basis whilst playing, be 100% involved in the game and the goal of winning, and at the same time not be distracted by external factors such as the watching crowds.

Model

Large, quadrangular and fixed in motivation, the Model is a predominantly blue/green figure, making it sensitive and receptive, with the one red aspect providing energy and drive. Its component parts are a Dominant and a Large Learning Triangle, a Projection Figure and a Small Talent Triangle. The red/green planet is alert, infused with nervous energy and a focal point within the figure. *Aspect Pattern Astrology* says that someone with a Model in their chart will have high aspirations and not be distracted by pessimism, and that their "centred persistence can give courage and hope to other people."

Marie Curie, Scientist

07.11.1867, 10:36 (standard time), Warsaw, Poland

The dominant structure of Marie Curie's chart is large and fixed. The Model is connected to a Kite and a Righteousness Rectangle. Neptune is the red/green planet, strongly placed in Aries in the 3rd house, stimulating the other planets (Sun, Uranus, Moon's Node) with its altruistic ideals. Curie was a chemist, physicist and pioneer of radioactivity. Through her research of uranium minerals, she discovered radium, and headed the first studies into the use of radioactive isotopes in the treatment of cancer. Neptune is connected to Uranus via the square, providing the energy to drive the high aspirations of the predominantly blue/green Model. Uranus is strongly placed by sign and house, symbolising the researcher who seeks and manifests new, ground-breaking insights.

Sun, Uranus and Moon's Node form the Small Talent Triangle within the Model, with the Node at the apex. Scorpio Sun at the top of the chart suggests full involvement of her will in tirelessly pursuing her researches alongside husband and fellow scientist Pierre. An 8th house Node suggests an awareness of and responsibility towards the needs of society, reflected in Curie's decision not to patent the process she discovered for isolating radium – ensuring that further research by the wider scientific community could continue. She was the first person to be awarded two Nobel Prizes, and the first woman professor at the University of Paris.

Recorder

The Recorder is a fixed quadrangular figure composed of all three aspect colours, but with an emphasis on the blue aspects which support its motivation for security. It is able to use the one red aspect to manifest and put to work the imaginative capacity of the blue and green aspects. Composed of a Search Triangle, a Small Talent Triangle and two Learning Triangles, it contains many possibilities. People with a Recorder are able to record and store what is observed in the environment, such as feelings, ideas, images and situations. For this they will utilise the Talent Triangle and Search Triangle in a quest to find what is hidden, or was previously unnoticed.

May

22.01.1977, 08:15, Amiens, France

May's Recorder dominates the upper hemisphere of a chart which has two additional Small Talent Triangles. Pluto is at the apex of the Talent Triangle in the Recorder, strongly placed on the 9th cusp. Her career has involved 9th house activities, such as teaching, lecturing and research as an art historian, but a still-developing inherent talent involves working with images. She is a photographer and combines the energies of strongly-placed Neptune and Pluto to record, store and exhibit images which others might overlook. May takes her camera to derelict buildings, ghost towns and shabby back streets to photograph and record what she sees there, and has recently taken part in an exhibition entitled *Metamorphosis*, making full use of Pluto.

Mars at the red/green corner behaves as an active, critical and sensitive observer. May physically seeks out places for the best shots and angles, often going into dilapidated buildings. However she does this with due care and caution; Mars is, after all, in Capricorn! Saturn's role in this figure is to ground and manifest what May observes and how she records the images. Many of her photographs have something special about them, their subject matter being real life objects and settings that could easily be ignored or passed by. Neptune at the blue/green corner of the Recorder is instrumental in directing her attention towards the often-hidden images she is drawn to working with.

Representative

The Representative is quadrangular and contains all three aspect colours. With a high blue/green ratio, it is imaginative, creative and idealistic. With only one red aspect, this figure may at times seem laid back, even lazy. In *Aspect Pattern Astrology*, the Hubers say that people with the Representative can absorb everything around them. They are alert but are able to step back into a stillness which can be seen as impersonal: "...this person is often initially misunderstood or not taken seriously, but he is patient and can wait until the time is right for an idea, a new way of life or a whole philosophy."

Bruno Huber, Astrologer and Psychologist

29.11.1930, 12:55, Zürich, Switzerland

Bruno Huber was a pioneer of astrology. He blended together the psychosynthesis of Roberto Assagioli with the best of traditional astrology to create what became known as the Huber Method of Astrological Psychology. He was an ambassador for this approach and, as described of the Representative, his work was at first misunderstood and not always taken seriously by some traditionally entrenched astrologers. For many years Bruno researched the aspect patterns in this book, bringing ground-breaking insights.

The Representative is pinned by Moon, Venus, Jupiter/Pluto and the Moon's Node. The component Large Talent Triangle is pinned by planets in water signs, providing a conduit for his sensitivity (Moon, Venus) and intelligence (Jupiter, intensified by conjunct Pluto). When Age Point was conjunct Jupiter/Pluto he began researching aspect patterns, a task which continued for the rest of his life. Bruno's empirical research always involved working with the charts of real people, drawing on contact planets Moon and Venus. He could easily engage and empathise with others when discussing issues arising from their charts, accompanied by the deep clarity and wisdom of Jupiter/Pluto. The Moon's Node at the red/green corner of the Representative is a sensitive point. The 2nd house was where Bruno had to defend and represent his ideas, philosophies and integrity as a pioneer of astrological psychology.

Bathtub

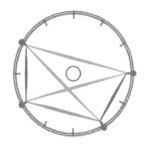

The Bathtub is a large fixed figure. What is contained within it will be hung on to and not readily relinquished. The sturdy blue aspects form the sides of the tub and the red square forms the base which provides energy and heats up the contents. A red/green combination of aspects produces sensitivity and it's not difficult to imagine hot water in the Bathtub bubbling and agitating. This can produce a constant level of stimulation and vulnerability for the individual, often to the extent of creating an ongoing level of fear and a chaotic approach to life. The inherent potential in this figure is found in learning from life's experiences.

Peter Sellers, Comedian and Actor

08.09.1925, 06:00, Southsea, UK

Peter Sellers is perhaps best known for his role as accident-prone Inspector Clouseau in the *Pink Panther* films. His chart contains a Bathtub and a Cradle; each has elements of insecurity for the individual if they step outside the figure's safe boundaries. The Bathtub is upside down, as if its contents are pouring away into the unconscious lower hemisphere. This suggests vulnerability and sensitive reactions to the collective, his audience. The green quincunxes pick up information which would be evaluated subjectively. With pinning Moon the highest planet in the chart, Sellers would want to shine and excel. He is described as difficult, demanding and erratic. He suffered from depression, associated with anxieties about his artistic and personal life. The doubts and fears inside the inverted Bathtub would be on view, especially to his audiences; he sought to hide them.

Sellers was known to have drunk heavily and used recreational drugs, which may have contributed to the anxiety, depression and series of heart attacks leading to his death. His 12th house Mercury/Neptune conjunction pins a corner of the Bathtub, symbolising an accessible escape route, via drink and drugs, away from the pressures of the sensitive green aspects. Aspecting Uranus in 7th, they might also be attributed to his skill as mimic and master of accents, perfected in the 1950s on BBC radio's surreal, ground-breaking *The Goon Show*, which set him on his career path.

Bijou

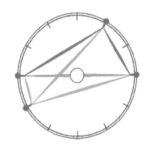

Bijou translated means "jewel" or "small and elegant". This quadrangular figure could be described as such because it has a certain lightness and attraction. Although fixed in motivation, it has a high quotient of green aspects. These make it flexible, alert and sensitive in the green side of the figure, but with the ability to be stable and create substance in the blue. People with a Bijou may try to balance out both sides, but will always combine elements of the predominantly blue/green aspect structure, focussing on ideas and the imagination. The red opposition is hidden inside, and points to an inner conflict which the individual has to resolve.

Joan Miró, Artist

20.04.1983, 11:30, Barcelona, Spain

The chart of Catalan artist Joan Miró has a strong vertical aspect structure, with a Bijou and an Irritation Rectangle. The high green quotient in both figures gives a fluid and sensitively alert chart. For Miró, ideas, thoughts and concepts would represent the security which is the motivation of quadrilateral figures. In the 1920s he was part of group of influential Spanish writers, poets, artists and film makers, reflected in the conjunction of transpersonal Neptune/Pluto on the 11th cusp at the Bijou's blue/green corner. He was a Surrealist who abhorred conventional painting techniques and experimented with automatic drawing to break free from more traditional techniques.

Surrealism was regarded by some as a revolutionary movement, and it is interesting to see Uranus, on the green corner of the Bijou, placed in the 4th house where it could potentially stir and shake up the expected norms. Uranus has only red and green aspects, making it receptive, reactive and restless. The opposition inside the Bijou spans the 3/9 Thinking Axis, pinned by Mercury and Saturn. This is the area of life where the inner conflict would be experienced and resolved. The inner realm of thoughts and ideas, which for Miró were part of the subconscious mind, were given outer expression through his painting, drawing, sculpture, murals and ceramics, no doubt helped by Saturn's strong placement in 3rd to provide the necessary material manifestation.

Magic Cap

A small figure on the periphery of the chart, the Magic Cap has the effect of making the wearer invisible. Fixed in motivation, with three green aspects facing outwards and two blue aspects which act as internal struts, the person is sensitive to others and likes to communicate. The two Information Triangles can absorb a wide variety of information; the two Small Learning Triangles are intent on learning new things. People with a Magic Cap can be easily influenced by the needs and feelings of others, often to the detriment of their own. They are reluctant to talk about themselves. The Hubers say of them, "He is a selfless server who no one can pin down."

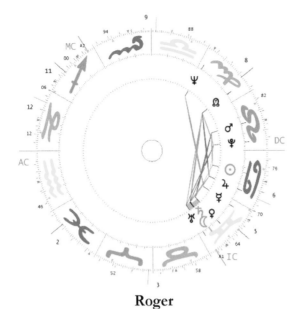

Roger

09.07.1942, 23:00, Lincoln, UK

The Magic Cap dominates Roger's chart. Its sensitivity and awareness is emphasised by the presence of a separate intersecting Information Triangle (Sun, Venus, Mars). Its receptiveness to the needs and feelings of others is emphasised by its position on the "You" side of an otherwise empty chart. The Magic Cap spans houses 4-8. Its area of activity is focussed where the pinning planets are found – on home and family in 4th, work and service in 6th, one-to-one encounters in 7th, with the Moon's Node indicating 8th house issues of social responsibility as a direction of growth. The rest of Roger's empty chart, including the "I" side, is of no interest or significance to him and he lives life mostly through contact with others.

Moon/Saturn in 4th in the Magic Cap symbolises a close, binding relationship with his mother and a need to stay close to the family home where security is found. Uranus on the IC, conjunct these planets but not part of the Magic Cap, was lived out in earlier life, when he travelled and worked abroad, eventually returning to live near the family home. Jupiter in Cancer in 6th finds expression, along with Cancerian Sun, in caring for various family members, almost a full-time job. He does, as the Hubers suggest, serve selflessly and his life is dominated by the needs of others and contact with them. He has no interest in his own needs, and says that if he were not caring for family he would do voluntary work.

Megaphone

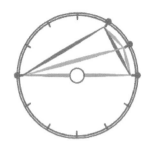

The Hubers describe the meaning of the Megaphone in *Aspect Pattern Astrology* saying, "We speak quietly into the narrow end and our voice suddenly fills the room. The other way round it works like the old-fashioned ear trumpet, as used in the past by the hard of hearing." The literal translation from German is a "whisper bag", suggesting a container for secrets or unexpressed ideals. This figure is about communication, both receiving and giving it. The area of the chart that it occupies is important and the high blue/green ratio of aspects highlight its idealistic, imaginative qualities with the red opposition holding and storing the energy of the planets which pin it.

Barack Obama, Politician

04.08.1961, 07:42, Honolulu, Hawaii, USA

Barack Obama's Megaphone (Mercury, Venus, Moon, Jupiter) dominates the chart's lower hemisphere. Its theme of communication is supported and emphasised by the presence of Mercury, which will seek expression relevant to its placement in the 6th house of service and work. Jupiter lies opposite, suggesting that a store of factual information and understanding, based on life experience, are held in a state of tension, ready to be expressed when needed. Venus and Moon will cooperate with Mercury in the taking in and giving out of communication, bringing sensitivity, charisma and a gentle touch.

Saturn conjunct Jupiter are tension rulers of the chart; these two don't necessarily sit well together – Dr. Doolittle's 'Push me – Pull you' creature comes to mind. They could be like driving with one foot on the accelerator and the other on the brake. Jupiter in Aquarius will want to go forward at its own pace with no holds barred; Saturn in Capricorn will provide a steadying influence but could act like a wet blanket. On the plus side, new ideas, projects and ideals will be formulated, responsibly and thoroughly underpinned and made manifest. A tension ruler acts like a filter through which passes everything experienced or expressed. Jupiter here could welcome all comers; Saturn will steadily suss out situations and provide a protective influence. This, in turn, will influence the communication coming from the Megaphone.

Oscillo

This is a sensitive quadrilateral with a high quotient of green aspects, giving the capacity to empathise with others. Its motivation includes learning and questing after an "ideal". Its highly attuned sensitivity means it reacts to the energies of people, places and situations. To oscillate is to be in constant movement between two points; likewise for the person with an Oscillo, who is well-balanced but in constant motion. In *Aspect Pattern Astrology* the Hubers describe the person with an Oscillo as "returning to previously settled matters to check they are OK… like a watchdog or supervisor for ongoing projects, developments or activities."

Auguste Rodin, Sculptor and Artist

12.11.1840, 12:00, Paris

Auguste Rodin's sculptures departed from traditional approaches. He aimed to create a realistic depiction of the human form using techniques which allowed the subject's character to shine through. He sought to convey emotion through textured surfaces, layering on the clay to build up a realistic representation. It is not difficult to imagine his Oscillo at work here: the constant movement, the to and fro checking of angles and perspectives of his work along with his heightened sensitivity to the energy and vibration of his subject.

Rodin's Oscillo appears upside down, balanced on a gyratory point at apex Pluto. Rather than the weight of this figure being at the base, the oscillations will be controlled from here. At this angle the Oscillo resembles a spinning plate on a pole. Although sensitive to the controversy surrounding his work, Rodin refused to change his style. Pinning Sun, Mars, Saturn and Pluto make a formidable lineup, helping him to stand his ground in the face of initial rejection of his techniques. Mars and Saturn on Balance Points, Pluto on 3rd cusp and stressed Scorpio Sun would not be easily intimidated. The Hubers say of the Oscillo, "In his phlegmatic single-mindedness, he is very patient and far-sighted, a lone searcher who manages to achieve his goal." Rodin's ability to capture the physical and intellectual essence of the human form is epitomised in *The Thinker*, and his work is highly regarded as a celebration of human emotion and character.

Stage

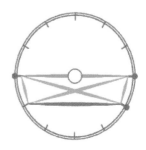

The Stage contains two green quincunxes crisscrossing inside like struts. This quadrilateral has fixed motivation but with four green aspects there is considerable flexibility within. Green aspects form two sides and there are green aspects inside. This is where the bulk of thinking, searching, doubting, questioning, sensitivity and awareness will take place. With theatrical connotations, the Stage is a base from which the individual can perform, and is the platform from which they can learn, understand and connect with others, using the green aspects to pick up all manner of messages and clues about human interaction and behaviour, with the blue aspect storing this information. In *Aspect Pattern Astrology* the Hubers say that people with this pattern "try to talk away differences and to create a unified picture."

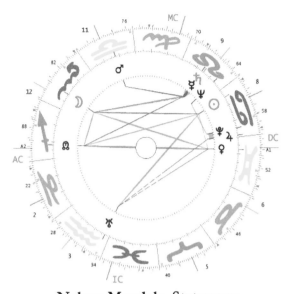

Nelson Mandela, Statesman

18.07.1918, 14:54, Umtata, South Africa

Nelson Mandela's chart contains a Stage pinned by Sun, Moon, Venus and the Moon's Node. The Stage is a relatively rare figure which can act like a bridge which connects opposing sides and viewpoints. It spans the chart and has the ability to resolve the opposition which it contains. Venus is opposite the Moon's Node, on the 6/12 house axis, which would suggest conflict on the theme of service and existence. However, the time of birth is unreliable, so caution is advised about seeing too much significance in this.

Drawing on both Sun and Moon, which connect the blue aspect of this figure, Mandela would have the capacity to use both rational (Sun/mind) and emotional (Moon) approaches to issues which call on the expression of the Stage. Venus adds discrimination and the ability to harmonise and build bridges. It is worth considering the role of the Moon's Node in this figure too. If the person has not consciously started to develop their activities and awareness of the house where this is positioned, it is quite likely that this part of the figure will act like a dumb note, not functioning – which is unlikely in the case of Mandela.

Striving Figure

Green Kite

The Striving Figure is a relatively rare quadrilateral, more inclined towards flexibility than fixity because of the high proportion of green, thinking aspects. These enclose the one red and one blue aspect, making the figure sensitive and receptive to external influences. The base, where the Information Triangle is found, is mobile rather than rigid, and the whole figure is dependent on the one blue sextile for stability and storage of information gathered. The sharply pointed apex, with its red/green aspects, is highly sensitised and the qualities of the planet here denote long term objectives. Although the person can aim high, with so many green aspects they may sometimes fall short of their goals.

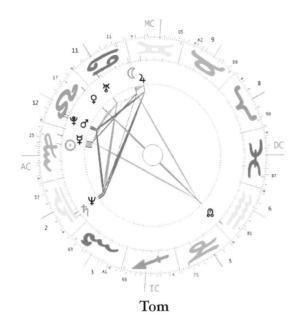

Tom

02.09.1953, 07:00, London, UK

Tom's Striving Figure sits across the 5/11 Relationship Axis in this predominantly blue/green chart. The relative lack of red "doing" aspects and the green-dominated Striving Figure suggest a thinker, someone who is aware and strives for perfection (Sun in Virgo). Tom describes himself as a perfectionist with a tendency to nitpicking. The Striving Figure is pinned at its base by Moon, Mercury and Venus. These personal planets indicate that this part of the figure is concerned with feelings, relating and communicating, reinforced by the figure's placement on the Relationship Axis. Tom is likely to be receptive to and aware of the needs of others, specifically his selected friends, as the base spans the 11th house of chosen friendships.

The path of growth lies in Tom becoming more aware of the 5th house, where the North Node is at the apex of the Striving Figure. Progress lies in connecting not only with the needs of those he chooses to relate to, but in being more open to the needs of people from all walks of life. Using the green aspects to bring greater awareness to what he does, he can strengthen the red opposition, the figure's backbone. With Venus in 11th at its base, the biggest step forward for Tom would be to consciously activate all matters relating to the 5th house and in doing so, fulfil the figure's potential. It should be borne in mind, though, that Tom is sensitive, and may require handling with kid gloves.

Surfer

Although quadrangular and security-motivated, the Surfer is alert and aware, able to adapt quickly to change. Like a windsurfing board upon which the surfer has to achieve balance and adjust rapidly to constantly changing motion, a person with a Surfer will recognise and respond to opportunities for change in the environment. This predominantly blue/green figure has one red aspect to energise and make manifest its creative and imaginative potential. The world sees the nervous energy of the red/green outer aspects; internally, the blue aspects provide firm support. In *Aspect Pattern Astrology* the Surfer is described as "very sensitive to the balance of power around him... his deep inner sense of justice forces him to support the underdog, as he always tries to make things fair."

Émile Zola, Novelist and Journalist

02.04.1840, 23:00, Paris, France

Émile Zola's chart is dominated by a Surfer. Pinned on one corner by a stellium of 5 strongly placed Aries planets, it has Jupiter riding high at the apex. Resembling a pennant, this planet receives all three aspect colours, helping the individual to maintain balance and stay in control as they ride the rough waters around them.

Zola risked his career when, in 1898, the famous headline "J'accuse…" was published on the front page of the Paris newspaper *L'Aurore*. In an open letter to the French President, Zola accused high officials in the French army of obstructing justice and of anti-semitism in what became known as the *Dreyfus Affair*. Army captain Alfred Dreyfus had been arrested and convicted of high treason for revealing military secrets to the Germans. Evidence was flimsy and although there was a traitor in the ranks, Dreyfus, a wealthy Jew, was chosen as scapegoat. His court martial was laced with dubious evidence to ensure a conviction. Zola's *J'accuse* letter demanding justice and fairness was published when his Age Point was on the Low Point of the 11th, opposite Sun and quincunx Venus in his Surfer. At the same time, his nodal Age Point was opposite the Surfer's apex planet Jupiter. Dreyfus was eventually exonerated in 1906.

Trampoline

Although quadrangular and fixed in motivation, the Trampoline embodies considerable flexibility with 3 green aspects which, according to *Aspect Pattern Astrology*, make it work "as if there was a green rubber sheet stretched over it." The green aspects form a surface which can be used to jump away from things, or bounce back towards them. Externally, people with a Trampoline appear sensitive. They are very perceptive and think convergently. The blue aspects offer a firm inner structure which is used when they act according to their high ideals. The one red aspect provides a strong base to work from. The Hubers say this figure is "an inveterate collector of knowledge which takes place on an intellectual level if the intelligence planets are present."

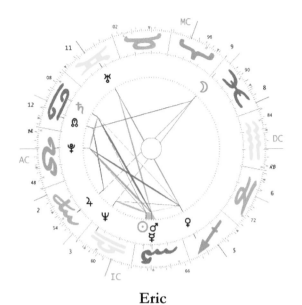

Eric

28.10.1944, 23:45, Lincoln, UK

Eric's Trampoline is pinned by 3 intelligence planets (Sun, Saturn, Mercury). Sun/Mercury/Mars are conjunct in intercepted Scorpio and Sun is at the apex of the attached Information Triangle. There is much potential here for collecting knowledge and using the intellect; Sun/Mercury connect with Saturn via one of the inner blue struts. Eric is not satisfied with superficial knowledge. Preferring to delve deeply into subjects which interest him, he will read and study in depth. Such activities go on at an inner level, reflecting the intercepted Scorpio planets, the fixed quality of the sign and of connected Saturn. The Hubers say of the Trampoline, "People with this figure do not exactly have much time for those around them, as they are never focussed on the outside." In Eric this is often so.

Eric is a pleasant, easy going person, the open "You" side of his chart between Moon and Venus emphasising his receptivity to others. If, however, he is attacked either physically or verbally, he will retaliate in no uncertain terms. The intercepted planets in Scorpio find expression via the red square aspect to Pluto on the AC. Pluto along with Saturn take a very firm stance and people who see him as laid back and quiet are often taken aback. But Venus will be instrumental in the Trampoline's bounce back afterwards, when harmony and equilibrium is restored.

Trawler

Vacuum Cleaner

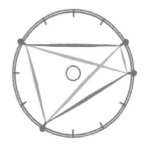

The Trawler is a large quadrangular figure with fixed motivation, emphasised by the long blue aspects which form its stable side walls. These are like finely polished surfaces, making it difficult for people to get inside and see what is going on. The semi-sextile is sensitive and busily acquires information, sucking it in by using the energy of the red aspect at the other end of this trawling basket and trapping it inside. The Trawler has a good learning ability, gathering and processing information using the green aspects. It behaves like someone with an always-empty rumbling stomach which needs to be filled with yet more data.

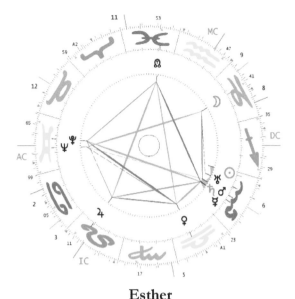

Esther

20.11.1895, 16:55, London, UK

Esther's Trawler is connected to several other figures. With the semi-sextile aimed at houses 5 and 6, it worked as described in *Aspect Pattern Astrology*: "...like a vacuum cleaner that points towards people and sucks them in as they come near." Esther was a caring person, willing to do a good turn to help out family, neighbours and church members. However, with a Trawler here people can be sucked in to its interior, and find it hard to get out. Esther knew a lot. She had to hand useful and sometimes irrelevant information which she would pass on, aiming to be helpful but often just confusing or irritating others. Venus in 5th and Mercury in 6th pin the semi-sextile, and she would dispense all manner of helpful hints (especially health-related) for family and friends. She had a certain charisma, power and authority, possibly related to Pluto at one end of the Trawler's square aspect.

As a young woman in the early 1920s Esther worked as a lady chauffeur, unusual at a time when this job was dominated by men. She wore a smart uniform with peaked cap, and drove a large convertible limousine. She chauffeured her boss, the owner of a London factory, all over Britain when her Age Point was conjunct Venus, picking up the Trawler. In later years, whenever a location in Britain was mentioned, she would inevitably have been there. Information and stories about the place she visited long ago would come pouring out as her Trawler dispensed its knowledge.

Pandora's Box

Pandora's Box is a rare figure. Being a five sided pentagon it is fixed in motivation. Encased in blue/red aspects, when viewed from the outside it can appear to approach life in a black/white, clear cut way. But inside there are sensitive green aspects, all of them long, searching quincunxes, making people with this figure long-term seekers, posing endless questions about life. For those outside, it's difficult to see inside the box because individuals with this figure can be inscrutable. If they were to open the box so others could see the contents, it is not so much that something bad or nasty might emerge, more that what goes on inside would be in sharp contrast to what was expected.

Imogen

22.08.1973, 16:08, Manchester, UK

Imogen's chart is complex, with many identifiable aspect figures. Most green aspects are enclosed within a large fixed structure, mainly bounded by blue aspects, suggesting outer calmness and stability, someone who appears pleasant and laid back. The Pandora's Box lies on its side across the horizontal axis, with Neptune at the top of its blue lid on the 12th house Low Point. If this lid were removed and the green aspects exposed, Imogen's rich inner world could become visible, which may surprise those who only see the surface. But this would firstly expose only the chart's "I" side, so it is Imogen herself who might initially discover more.

Looking inside the box, it becomes apparent that Imogen is attuned to and interested in imaginative, creative pursuits which could involve healing, music or mysticism. Jupiter on one corner of the lid offers expanded awareness and interests. Venus/Pluto on the other corner, well-aspected with all 3 colours and visually focal in the chart, suggest an intensity and charisma that Imogen may not be aware of. Mars at one corner of the base is stressed before the 5th cusp; its quincunx to Venus/Pluto may add to the intensity, especially in the area of relationships. On the other corner, Saturn in the 7th house contributes grounding, stabilising and practical application. Imogen is training to teach the Alexander Technique, a therapy for improving mental and physical function.

Alphabetical Index

Pictorial Index

Red Figures

Achievement
Triangle 8

Achievement
Square 10

Blue Figures

Large Talent
Triangle 12

Small Talent
Triangle 14

Red and Blue Figures

Ambivalence
Triangle 16

Cradle
18

Kite
20

Righteousness
Rectangle 22

Red and Green Figures

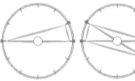

Irritation
Triangle 24

Irritation
Rectangle 26

Blue and Green Figures

Information
Triangle 28

Projection
Triangle 30

Search
Triangle 32

Three Colours Equal

Decorative
Figure 34

Dominant
Learning 36

Large/Med/Small
Learning 38

Shield
40

Streamer
42

Telescope
44

Trapeze
46

UFO
48

Three Colours Most Red

Animated
Figure 50

Arena
52

Double
Ambivalence 54

Provocative
Figure 56

Three Colours Most Blue

Detective
58

Model
60

Recorder
62

Representative
64

Three Colours Most Green

Bathtub
66

Bijou
68

Magic Cap
70

Megaphone
72

Oscillo
74

Stage
76

Striving
Figure 78

Surfer
80

Trampoline
82

Trawler
84

Three Colours Blue Green

Pandora's Box
86

Resources

Astrological Psychology Association

A MODERN APPROACH to SELF-AWARENESS and PERSONAL GROWTH

Astrology is now recognised as providing a valuable tool for the development of self awareness and human potential. Bruno and Louise Huber researched and developed astrological psychology over many years, combining the best of astrology with Roberto Assagioli's psychosynthesis.

DIPLOMA IN ASTROLOGICAL PSYCHOLOGY
   Learn astrological psychology
   Understand yourself and help others

FOUNDATION COURSES IN ASTROLOGY
   The basics of astrology

MEMBERSHIP
   Community of interest, magazine, discounts...

ONLINE RESOURCES
   Prospectus, bookshop, consultants, forum...

www.astrologicalpsychology.org

Enquiries: enquiries@astrologicalpsychology.org

Teaching Astrological Psychology since 1983

APA Bookshop
Books and APA publications related to the Huber Method.
Linda Tinsley, APA Bookshop
70 Kensington Road, Southport PR9 0RY, UK
Tel: 00 44 (0)1704 544652, Email: lucindatinsley@tiscali.co.uk

---

Huber Chart Data Service
Provides colour-printed Huber-style charts and chart data.
Richard Llewellyn, Huber Chart Data Service
PO Box 29, Upton, Wirral CH49 3BG, UK
Tel: 00 44 (0)151 606 8551, Email: r.llewellyn@btinternet.com

---

Software for Huber-style Charts
AstroCora, MegaStar, Regulus
On CD: Elly Gibbs Tel: 00 44 (0)151-677-0779
            Email: software.huber@btinternet.com
Download: Cathar Software Website: www.catharsoftware.com

Publications on Astrological Psychology

The Cosmic Egg Timer
by Joyce Hopewell & Richard Llewellyn

Introduces astrological psychology. Use your own birth chart alongside this book and gain insights into the kind of person you are, what makes you tick, and which areas of life offer you the greatest potential.

Aspect Pattern Astrology

Understanding motivation through aspect patterns. Essential reference work. The aspect pattern reveals the structure and basic motivations of our consciousness. Over 45 distinct aspect figures are identified, each with its own meaning.

The Planets and their Psychological Meaning

Shows how the positions of the planets are fundamental to horoscope interpretation. They represent basic archetypal qualities present in everyone, giving clues to psychological abilities and characteristics, growth and spiritual development.

Astrological Psychosynthesis

Astrology as a Pathway to Growth. Bruno Huber's introduction to this holistic approach to astrology and Assagioli's psychosynthesis, following the premise that the soul is at the root of all developmental processes. Focus on intelligence, integration, relationships.

Moon Node Astrology

Combines psychological understanding with the concept of reincarnation, bringing a new astrological focus on the shadow personality and the individual's evolutionary process. Includes the psychological approach used with the Moon's Nodes and the Node Chart.

* Books by Bruno & Louise Huber except where authors otherwise indicated.

A Modern Approach to Self Awareness and Personal Growth

LifeClock

The horoscope is seen as a clock for the person's lifetime, with the Age Point indicating their age as the 'time' on the clock. Those trying it invariably find significant correspondences between indications in their birth chart and meaningful events in their lives.

Transformation

Astrology as a Spiritual Path. Describes processes of transformation and personal/spiritual growth as natural stages in human development, related to astrological indicators in the birth chart. New material on Dynamic Houses, Stress Planets, House Chart, Integration Chart.

The Living Birth Chart
by Joyce Hopewell

Aims to provide insight into the full power of the Huber Method and give a feel for its practical use, with numerous examples and exercises enabling the reader to experience the approach for themselves.

AstroLog I: Life and Meaning

There is now a substantial body of experience in the 'Huber Method' documented in the German-language magazine *AstroLog*. First selection of articles translated into English, on astrological psychology and its relevance to life and its meaning. Various authors.

AstroLog II: Family, Relationships & Health

The second selection of articles, by various authors including the Hubers, translated from *AstroLog*. Their subjects relate to astrological psychology and its use in the context of family members, personal relationships and individual health.

Published by HopeWell, PO Box 118, Knutsford, Cheshire WA16 8TG, UK

Lightning Source UK Ltd.
Milton Keynes UK
UKHW051830070122
396783UK00006B/162